Bird Families

by Helen Frost

Consulting Editor: Gail Saunders-Smith, Ph.D.
Consultant: Ilze Balodis, Institute for Field
Ornithology, University of Maine at Machias

Pebble Books

an imprint of Capstone Press
Mankato, Minnesota

Pebble Books are published by Capstone Press
818 North Willow Street, Mankato, Minnesota 56001
http://www.capstone-press.com

Library of Congress Cataloging-in-Publication Data
Frost, Helen, 1949–
Bird families/by Helen Frost.
    p. cm.—(Birds)
    Includes bibliographical references and index.
    Summary: Describes where and how various species of birds nest, including
sites in tree branches, in hollow trees, near water, and on cliffs.
    ISBN 0-7368-0224-X
1. Birds—Behavior—Juvenile literature. 2. Familial behavior in animals—Juvenile
literature. [1. Birds—Nests.] I. Title. II. Series: Frost, Helen, 1949– Birds.
QL698.3.F75 1999
598´.1563—dc21   98-45444
                                                                              CIP
                                                                              AC

Note to Parents and Teachers

The Birds series supports national science standards related to
the diversity and unity of life. This book describes where and how
different species of bird families nest. The photographs support
early readers in understanding the text. The repetition of words
and phrases helps early readers learn new words. This book also
introduces early readers to subject-specific vocabulary words,
which are defined in the Words to Know section. Early readers
may need assistance to read some words and to use the Table of
Contents, Words to Know, Read More, Internet Sites, and
Index/Word List sections of the book.

Table of Contents

Nesting Alone 5
Nesting Together 13

Note to Parents and Teachers . . . 2
Words to Know 22
Read More 23
Internet Sites 23
Index/Word List 24

Some bird families
nest alone.

Northern cardinal families nest alone on tree branches.

Canada goose families
nest alone near water.

Woodpecker families
nest alone inside trees.

Some bird families
nest together.

14

Cliff swallow families
nest together on cliffs.

Great blue heron families nest together in tall trees.

Pigeon families nest together on buildings.

Atlantic puffin families
nest together near water.

Words to Know

Atlantic puffin—a black and white seabird with a short neck and a colorful beak

Canada goose—a gray-brown bird with a black head, a black tail, and black legs

cliff swallow—a brown and white bird with orange-red cheeks and a white or orange-red forehead

great blue heron—a gray-blue bird with a long bill, long legs, and a long neck

northern cardinal—a songbird with a crest of feathers on the head and black coloring around the bill; male cardinals are bright red and female cardinals are mostly brown with a red crest.

pigeon—a plump bird that is mainly gray; many pigeons live in cities.

woodpecker—a bird with a strong, pointed bill; woodpeckers use their bills to drill holes in trees.

Read More

Boring, Mel. *Birds, Nests, and Eggs.* Young Naturalist Field Guides. Milwaukee: Gareth Stevens, 1998.

Jenkins, Priscilla Belz. *A Nest Full of Eggs.* Let's-Read-and-Find-Out Science. New York: HarperCollins, 1995.

Weidensaul, Scott. *National Audubon Society First Field Guide. Birds.* New York: Scholastic, 1998.

Internet Sites

All about Birds
http://www.enchantedlearning.com/subjects/birds

Classroom Bird Watch
http://birdsource.cornell.edu/classroomBS/index.html

Fledgling Corner—Birding for Kids
http://birding.miningco.com/msubmenu13.htm

Index/Word List

alone, 5, 7, 9, 11
Atlantic puffin, 21
branches, 7
buildings, 19
Canada goose, 9
cliffs, 15
cliff swallow, 15
families, 5, 7, 9, 11,
  13, 15, 17, 19, 21
great blue heron, 17

nest, 5, 7, 9, 11, 13,
  15, 17, 19, 21
northern cardinal, 7
pigeon, 19
some, 5, 13
together, 13, 15, 17,
  19, 21
tree, 7, 11, 17
water, 9, 21
woodpecker, 11

Word Count: 60
Early-Intervention Level: 8

Editorial Credits

Colleen Sexton, editor; Steve Weil/Tandem Design, cover designer;
  Kimberly Danger and Sheri Gosewisch, photo researchers

Photo Credits

Bill Johnson, 8
Jay Ireland & Georgienne Bradley, cover
Joe McDonald, 10
John Gerlach/Tom Stack & Associates, 4
Robert McCaw, 12, 16
Root Resources/Anthony Mercieca, 1
Visuals Unlimited/Tom J. Ulrich, 6; William J. Weber, 14;
  Louie Bunde, 18; John Gerlach, 20

23

10-5/05

WITHDRAWN

2 2